Patrick Gaffikin

DEDICATION

This book is dedicated to my nephews and nieces – Eamon, Paul, Catherine, Claire, Laura and Ryan – and my grandnieces Kirsten, Ana, Sara and Sophia.

– Patrick Gaffikin

First published in 2008 by
Appletree Press Ltd
The Old Potato Station
14 Howard Street South
Belfast BT7 1AP

Tel: + 44 (0) 28 90 24 30 74
Fax: + 44 (0) 28 90 24 67 56
Email: reception@appletree.ie
Web-site: www.appletree.ie

Copyright © Appletree Press Ltd, 2008
Text by Patrick Gaffikin
Photographs © author's own except where acknowledged in the text and the following:
© istockphoto.com / Yves Grau (p. 4)
© istockphoto.com / Heiko Grossman (p. 36)

Ulster Museum photographs reproduced with the kind permission of the Trustees of the National Museums and Galleries of Northern Ireland.

All rights reserved. Printed in China. No part of this publication may be reproduced, stored in a retrieval system or transmitted in any form or by any means, electronic, mechanical, photocopying, recording or otherwise, without the prior permission of the copyright holder.

A catalogue record for this book is available from the British Library.

Irish Fossils

ISBN-13: 978 1 84758 073 3

9 8 7 6 5 4 3 2 1

AP3519

CONTENTS

Introduction	5
The Geological Time Scale	18
How Do Fossils Form?	21
Why Are Fossils Important?	25
A Guide to Fossil-hunting	31
Fossils Found in Ireland	37
Sponges	39
Corals	43
Arthropods (Trilobites and Ostracods)	49
Brachiopods	57
Bryozoans	63
Molluscs (Gastropods, Bivalves, Ammonoids and Belemnites)	67
Echinoderms (Sea-urchins and Crinoids)	83
Graptolites	91
Experiments to Try At Home	94
Acknowledgements	96
Further Reading	96

Jurassic ammonite

INTRODUCTION

The geological diversity of Ireland

The Ireland that we see today is the product of a long journey through time and space. This story covers almost two billion years of the Earth's history, taking us from south polar regions, through equatorial zones to our present position. Geologists are able to interpret clues in the rocks that tell of former oceans and mountain building events. Such oceans once separated the north of Ireland which, together with Scotland, was actually associated with lands that now form part of North America while the south of Ireland, together with England and Wales, lay on the other side of this now lost Iapetus Ocean. Past mountain ranges in Ireland have included one on the scale of the Himalayas, dating from the closure of this ocean and caused by the collision of tectonic plates from which our Earth's crust is formed. It is the movement of these plates which has taken us through so many climatic zones (although the Earth's climate itself has also varied enormously) – our rocks contain evidence of past deserts, glaciers, deep oceans and shallow tropical seas. This diversity of environments explains the great range of rock types and the remarkable representation of geological periods found in Ireland. As many of these rocks also contain evidence of past life of the planet, we should not be surprised that Ireland also hosts a great diversity of fossils.

What are fossils?

Many people when they hear the word 'fossil' associate it with mysterious bones, or the remains of plants or animals which lived on the Earth many years ago. Hopefully as the reader progresses through this pocket guide the 'mystery' about fossils will be replaced by a better understanding.

It was in 1546 that the word 'fossil' first appeared in the title of a book – *De natura fossilium* (translated as: 'On the nature of fossils') – by a German medical doctor called Georgius Agricola. The word is derived from the Latin *fossilis,* which means 'something dug up'. When first used it referred to geological specimens generally – rocks, minerals and fossils. It was even originally used for archaeological artefacts.

However, its usage soon was restricted to describe what officially today are termed 'fossils' – ancient shells, bones and other remnants preserved in rocks. The generally accepted definition of a **fossil** is: **the remains or traces of an ancient animal or plant which have**

been preserved in rock. The word 'ancient' is used in the sense of geological time. So, for example, the skeleton of say a horse, which died 5, 10 or even 100 years ago would not be described as a fossil. Neither would the 3,000-year-old Egyptian mummy, exhibited in the Ulster Museum be regarded as a fossil. Palaeontology – derived from the Greek words *palaios* + *ontos* + *logos* meaning, respectively, 'ancient', 'being' and 'discourse' – is used to describe the branch of geology dealing with the study of fossils.

How long have people known about fossils?

People have known about fossils for as long as they have been looking at rocks. The Stone Age people, who lived in Ireland over 4,500 years ago, would have undoubtedly come across them. What exactly they thought about them will never be known but folklore has it that, even in historical times, fossils were used as charms to 'cure' the sick and for 'protection' for the healthy.

Certain oyster fossils for example were used to 'cure' joint-pains because they look something like an arthritic toe or finger. Ammonites, thought to be petrified snakes and sometimes called 'snake stones', were used for 'protection' against snake bites while belemnites, considered to have been deposited on Earth during thunder storms, gave 'protection' against lightning strikes. In fact belemnites used to be called 'thunderbolts'.

What are the oldest fossils found in Ireland?
These are about 550 million years old and consist of fan-like impressions, found in slates at Bray Head in Co. Wicklow. Their scientific name is *Oldhamia antiqua* and at the time of their discovery they were thought to be the oldest fossils in the world.

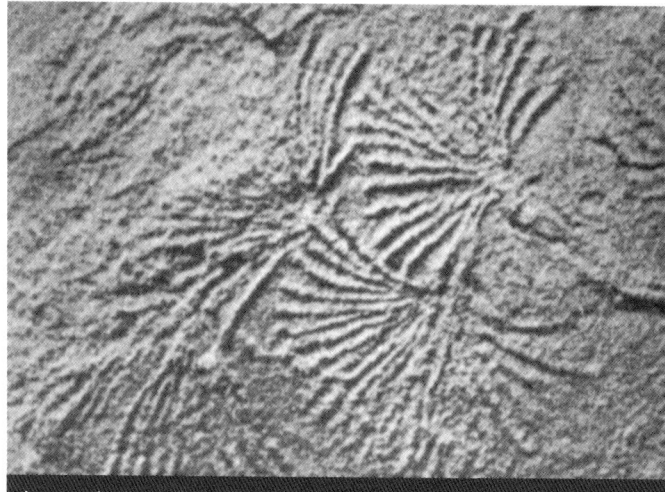

Impressions, called trace fossils, of *Oldhamia antiqua*, found in rocks at Bray Head. [Photo printed with the kind permission of the Geology Department, Trinity College, Dublin.]

Introduction

Some of the oldest known fossils in N. Ireland are 450 million years old and occur in mudstones in a stream near Acton, Co. Armagh. They are minute fossils – known as microfossils because of their size – called conodonts, which are believed to have come from now extinct primitive marine fish-like animals.

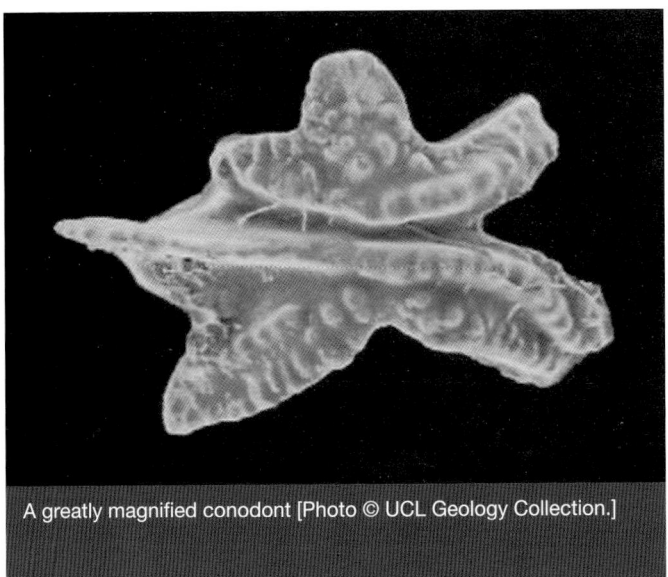

A greatly magnified conodont [Photo © UCL Geology Collection.]

Why do fossils have unusual names?

Fossils have 'general' names like sponges, corals, trilobites, bivalves, ammonites etc. But individual species, in order to distinguish them from other specimens, have a two-part name. The first name is called the genus and the second name is called the species. Just as each person has an individual name and a surname, we could look on the scientific names of fossils in a similar way – except with fossils the 'surname' is written first (the genus) and the 'individual name' (the species) is written second. Take the case of an oyster bivalve fossil called *Gryphaea arcuata*. Here the genus is *Gryphaea* and the species is *arcuata*.

Rocks that contain fossils
– and those that don't

Fossils are almost exclusive to rocks we call sedimentary rocks – rocks such as limestone, chalk (a very pure form of limestone), shale, mudstone, greensand, siltstone and sandstone. All these rocks occur in Ireland. Igneous rocks – that is rocks formed from molten rock we call magma – are virtually unfossiliferous. For example you would never find fossils in any kind of granite, an igneous rock which formed entirely underground. Very occasionally plant fossils in the form of moulds of trunks, roots and branches of ancient trees

The fossil oyster *Gryphaea arcuata* which was found on the Waterloo shore, about 1 km north of Larne, Co. Antrim.

have been found in the igneous rock called basalt. The other main group of rocks – metamorphic rocks – may sometimes yield fossils if these were formed from metamorphosed (altered) rocks that were originally sedimentary. For example, the metamorphic rock, called hornfels, which was formed by the action of heat on sedimentary rock shale can be seen at Portrush, Co. Antrim and contains ammonite fossils of Jurassic age. These fossils can be viewed and photographed but must not be collected.

Examples of ammonite fossils in the metamorphic rock called hornfels on the shore, east of Lansdowne Terrace at Portrush, Co. Antrim. [Photo: Mr. P. Millar, Belfast Geologists' Society.]

How will I know if I have found a fossil?

If a specimen is found and you are in doubt as to whether it is a fossil, note the following:

- If it is embedded in rock and looks like part of a plant or animal then the chances are it is a fossil. Some exceptions to this are so called 'pseudo fossils' – for example dendrites, concretions or mineral nodules. These are quite rare, however, in Ireland. Flint nodules are common in the Antrim Chalk but these do not have fossil-like structures.

Left to Right (a) Concretions – one of their rare occurrences is on the Waterloo shore, near Larne. (b) Marcasite (a form of iron sulphide) nodules (c) 'Fresh' shells, too recent to be regarded as fossils.

Irish Fossils

- Shells found on a beach may or may not be fossils. If the specimen is of an extinct animal – for example an ammonite, a belemnite or a *Gryphaea* – then it would be a fossil.
- Many fossils have undergone some degree of alteration and so, for instance, if a shell found on a beach looks very 'fresh' the likelihood is it is not a fossil. Another indicator of this can be if they occur in abundance. However, on occasion, very fresh-looking fossils can occur in abundance at selected localities.
- Ask a geologist or a palaeontologist for their opinion if still in doubt.

Example of a pseudo fossil. It looks like a plant fossil but it is really a mineral with tree-like branching. It was found at Cloghfin Port, Islandmagee, Co. Antrim by Dr. N. Moles, Q.U.B.

What type of fossils am I likely to see in Ireland?

Most of the fossils you can see in Ireland are of invertebrate marine animals that lived millions of years ago and which had some hard parts (e.g. shells). Although plant fossils do occur, they are not as common. Microfossils, that is ones that could only be studied with a microscope, are very abundant in Ireland but are not appropriate for the beginner in this field. This guide will concentrate on fossils that can be seen without a microscope.

Fossils from most of the geological periods occur in Ireland – ranging from the Bray trace fossils, approximately 550 million years old (Late Pre-Cambrian), to the very recent fossils of the extinct Irish 'Elk', some 10,000 years old, found on the shore of Larne Lough, Co. Antrim, Ballybetagh Bog, Co. Dublin and elsewhere.

How do we know the age of a particular fossil?

Determining absolute ages in geology involves radiometric dating. Fossils are usually found in sedimentary rocks which can also contain rock-material of a contemporaneous igneous origin – for example volcanic ash – including traces of radioactive elements which enable a radiometric date to be established. So the age of the sediment,

Irish Fossils

An example of a plant fossil (the genus *Lepidodendron*). It is around 300 million years old and was found at Carrickmore, near Ballycastle, Co. Antrim. The coin is 2.5 cm in diameter. [Photo: Mr. P. Millar, Belfast Geologists' Society.]

and hence the age of the fossil in it, can be found (both ages are the same). If the same type of fossil turns up elsewhere then the age of the host rock will, in all probability, be the same.

Relative dating however relies on the relationship between rocks as they naturally occur in the countryside. Nearly all fossils occur in rocks which were originally sediments (mud, sand etc.) and are therefore called sedimentary. They typically formed in layers, building up progressively with the lowest such layers being the oldest while the uppermost are the youngest (unless subsequent earth movements have inverted them). This principle can be used to provide relative ages for the rocks and hence for the fossils they contain. Such an approach may also be used to provide relative dates from an outcrop where the geological age is known to one where it is unknown. For example, a diagnostic fossil found in known Carboniferous rocks at site A is also found at a new exposure at site B then the rocks at site B must also be Carboniferous in age.

Trace fossils

In addition to fossils of plant and animal remains, other evidence of animal life in particular may be found in rocks. Examples could include footprints, trails and burrows. These signs of former life are known as trace fossils.

Infilled burrows, Portmuck, Co. Antrim, *Thalassinoides* spp.

THE GEOLOGICAL TIME SCALE

Geological unit of time [1]	Commencing – million years ago (duration – million years) [3]	Main environment and rocks in Ireland	Main macrofossil groups
Recent	0.01	Forests, grassland, peatland, dunes.	
Quaternary	1.8 (1.79)	Ice sheets with intervening warm periods. Glacial till, sand and gravel deposits.	Rare mammoth and musk ox remains.
Neogene [3]	23 (21.2)	Erosion. Clay, sand and lignite deposited in basins.	Poorly preserved fossil woods.
Palaeogene [3]	65 (42)	Volcanic activity in NE Ireland. Basalt, granite and laterite soils.	Plant imprints.
Cretaceous	145 (80)	Warm shallow seas. Sandstone and white limestone.	Ammonites, nautiloids, belemnites, gastropods, bivalves, sponges, brachiopods, echinoids.
Jurassic	200 (55)	Warm shallow seas. Mudstone and limestone.	Ammonites, nautiloids, belemnites, gastropods, bivalves, crinoids, rare ichthyosaurs and plesiosaurs.
Triassic	251 (51)	Desert conditions followed by extensive periodic shallow water. Sandstone, mudstone and salt beds.	Animal tracks of reptiles and scorpions.

Period	Age (Ma)	Geology	Fossils
Permian	299 (48)	Erosion of uplands then shallow seas. Minor series of agglomerate, sandstone and limestone.	Very limited source material.
Carboniferous	359 (60)	Complex alteration between marine, deltaic and terrestrial conditions. Limestone, sandstone, shale, and coal.	Tree and plant imprints (coalfields). Fish teeth, trilobites, corals, brachiopods, goniatites, nautiloids, gastropods, bivalves, crinoids.
Devonian	416 (57)	Deserts with partial marine conditions in south. Sandstone, mudstone, basalt, granite.	Tetrapod tracks
Silurian	443 (27)	Deep marine sediments. Sandstone and shale. Limited shallow water mudstones and sandstones.	Graptolites
Ordovician	488 (45)	Deep marine sediments. Sandstone and shale. Limited shallow water mudstones and sandstones. Volcanic activity.	Bivalves, gastropods, brachiopods, trilobites, graptolites.
Cambrian	542 (54)	Marine continental shelf. Sandstone and slate.	Sparse trace fossils
Pre-Cambrian	4500 – formation of the earth		Very rare fossil traces from transitional Pre-Cambrian – Cambrian. Otherwise absent.

1. these are 'periods' with exceptions of Pre-Cambrian (Supereon) and Recent (epoch) 2. there is no complete agreement on these dates – they are amended periodically on the basis of new evidence 3. the Neogene and Palaeogene Periods were combined into the Tertiary Era.

Examples of pyritised ammonites (both of the genus *Promicroceras*) from the Lias Clay (Jurassic) in Co. Antrim. These fossils could have been formed in the way illustrated on p. 22. The brassy-coloured iron sulphide mineral, called iron pyrites, would have replaced the calcium carbonate of the original shell. The corrugations seen here are termed 'ribs'. In the last chamber the body of the ammonite resided, attached by muscles to the shell, and from its mouth a number of tentacles or arms protruded. [Photo: Robin Reid, England.]

HOW DO FOSSILS FORM?

If you find a fossil then consider yourself lucky – the majority of past animals and plants which lived in the past did not become fossils or, if they did, have not survived. Hence the fossil record only gives us a very incomplete picture of ancient life. The remains of most organisms were destroyed quickly by natural processes, decay or were simply consumed by predators.

Soft-bodied animals like worms and jellyfish, having no bony skeleton, usually decomposed rapidly in both terrestrial and aquatic conditions, and so their remains are not ordinarily preserved. Similarly the leaves, buds and flowers of plants are not commonly found as fossils. Such animals and plants often leave no record of their existence except, occasionally, in the form of imprints.

Animals with hard parts such as a skeleton or shell and plants such as trees with hard and massive trunks, have a better chance of being preserved. If they are buried quickly they can escape natural erosion and, in the course of time, may become preserved as fossils. Under water, sediments accumulate universally in the form of layers or beds and these readily cover the remains of organisms, thus facilitating their preservation as fossils. On land, where the accumulation of sediment is often more intermittent, the remains of animals and plants are more rarely entombed in sediment and hence have little chance of being fossilised – except in river laid deposits or in lakes. Most dinosaur fossils, for instance, are from river laid sediments.

How Fossils can Form

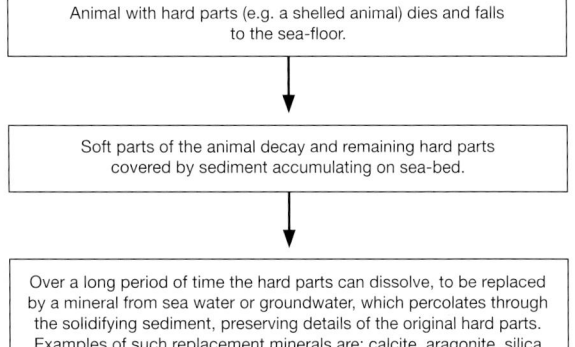

Fossils can also form in a number of other ways including:

- loss of all material except for the carbon content – this is called carbonisation and can result in the preservation of fossil plants associated with coal deposits;
- freezing can preserve even soft tissue as with mammoths found in Siberia;
- in amber where plants and especially insects are trapped in the hardened resin of ancient trees;
- in tar pits or peat bogs where the oxygen-poor conditions inhibit decomposition;
- as impressions in sediment where rapid burial in oxygen-poor conditions can result in details of organisms with no hard parts being preserved.

General points about the formation of fossils:

- Most fossils are formed in sediment accumulating under water. Since most of the water on our planet is sea water, most fossils form in marine conditions. Less commonly, fossils can also be formed in deltas, swamps and in (fresh water) lakes and rivers.
- When a living thing dies its soft parts are the first to decay, and this usually happens very rapidly. Hence soft parts are only very rarely preserved.
- The majority of fossils are formed from

organisms with some hard parts.
- The way sediment is deposited on dry land does not usually provide favourable conditions for the preservation of fossils.
- Hominids, which could loosely be described as having both human- and ape-like characteristics, and flying life forms such as insects, birds and pterosaurs are relatively rare as fossils.

WHY ARE FOSSILS IMPORTANT?

Fossil fuels

While no longer necessarily showing obvious signs of their origin, modern 'fossil fuels' are derived from the remains of former organisms. Examples include coal, which is the preserved remains of ancient vegetation which has been buried, compressed and converted into coal. In Ireland a coal field (now no longer working) can be found at Ballycastle, Co. Antrim, the coal series being Carboniferous in age – a period from which many coal deposits date throughout the world. 'Brown coal' or lignite (a poor grade coal) occurs around the southern part of Lough Neagh and near Ballymoney, Co. Antrim.

Oil is thought to have been formed from floating microscopic plants and animals called plankton which, millions of years ago, fell to the sea-bed then became buried and sealed within sedimentary rocks where they were altered by heat and pressure. Too much heat and the oil is converted to natural gas. Productive gas fields occur offshore around Ireland at Kinsale, Co. Cork and the more recently discovered Corrib field off the west coast.

In the search for oil and gas

Microfossils are very important during exploratory drilling for oil and gas as they can be used to identify rock sequences within and between boreholes. In fact, fossils have their chief practical use in the preliminary stages of the search for new oilfields and in other types of geological exploration.

Other commercial uses

The Co. Antrim Chalk is used as a source of lime and, to a lesser degree, formerly as a building stone. This Chalk is formed chiefly from tiny fossilised calcareous plates (known as coccoliths) from algae called coccolithophorids.

Portland Roach Limestone, from southern England, is full of fossil cavities which enhance its appearance and it is used as a building stone – an example of its use in Belfast is as a facing stone on the Cecil Ward Building, 4-10 Linenhall Street.

Actual fossil specimens also have a commercial value. The obvious modern use is their sale by specialist dealers but there are other older uses. Examples include: (1) the use of amber (fossil tree-resin) as trade goods and jewellery since at least the Bronze Age; (2) the use of powdered fossil bones and teeth in Chinese medicine, dating back centuries and (3) the making of jewellery from jet, which is a special form of carbonised wood.

A greatly magnified image of a coccolithophore whose plates help make up chalk. [Photo © UCL Geology Collection]

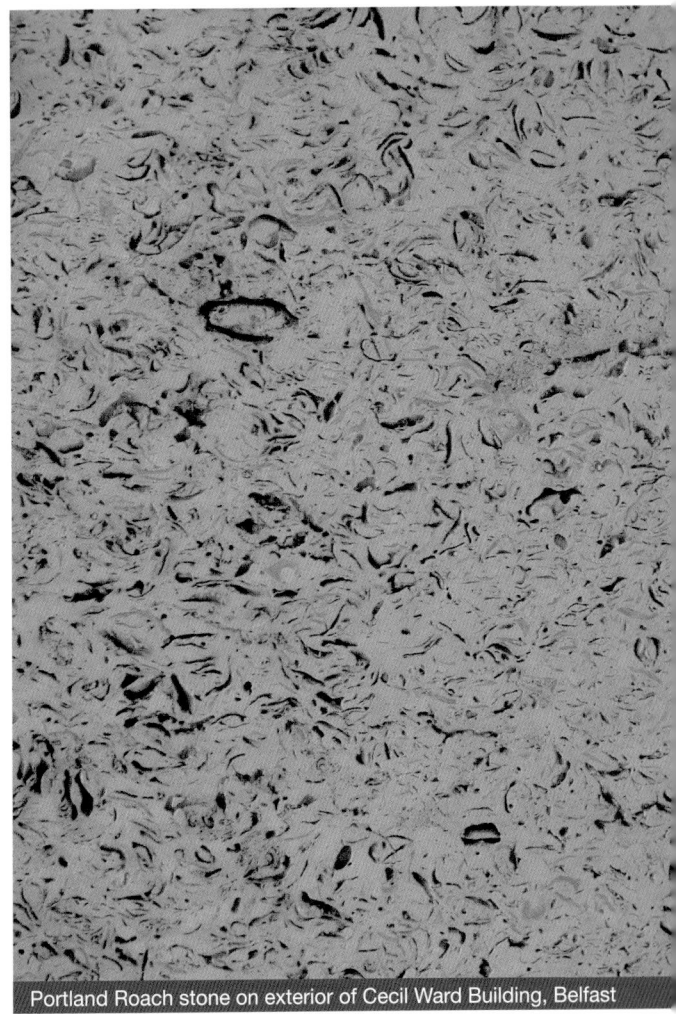

Portland Roach stone on exterior of Cecil Ward Building, Belfast

Understanding life

Fossils provide a picture of past life on Earth. We can tell, for example, that life originated on our planet in the sea about 3,500 million years ago because marine blue-green algae fossils are of this age. Fossils also show that the first multi-cellular (complex) animals appeared about 640 million years ago. Fossils tell us of extinct life forms such as trilobites, graptolites, ammonoids, belemnites and dinosaurs. They also provide information on the evolution of, and relationships between, the great diversity of life on planet Earth.

Geological uses
- Dating rocks

Recognition and identification of fossils is routine work for many geologists. Such evidence provides information on the age of the rocks being studied and allows correlation between rock series containing identical fossils, which may occur some considerable distance apart, even on different continents.

The most useful fossils for dating and correlating rocks are those of species which only lived for a relatively short geological time, were widely distributed throughout the Earth and would be quite easily recognisable. Ammonoid and graptolite fossils, for instance, fulfil these requirements.

Fossils also provide us with windows on the past as they, together with the rock in which they are found, contain evidence of the environmental conditions in which the organisms lived and how the rocks originated.

A GUIDE TO FOSSIL-HUNTING

Remember that fossils are a finite resource. Some types are abundant but others are rare. Similarly some sites hold large quantities of fossils or are eroding rapidly (leading to the loss of the fossils) while others are stable or hold very few fossils. Where and how you collect must be informed by such information. If in doubt, do not collect.

There are a number of codes of conduct covering fossil collecting e.g. www.jncc.gov.uk/pdf/Fossilcollectingpolicy.pdf

In summary

- Seek permission of landowners to enter private land and collect fossils.
- Always collect from loose material (e.g. stones on a beach or slipped material from rock faces).
- A number of important geological sites, in Northern Ireland and the Republic of Ireland, are designated Areas of Special Scientific Interest or National Heritage Areas. No collecting is permitted at these sites. Please photograph material.
- Unusual or rare fossils should always be shown to relevant professionals e.g. geology staff at the nearest museum.

- Document your finds with information on site name, position of fossils (e.g. grid reference and level found), date and finder's name.
- Photography offers an alternative to collecting, especially at sensitive localities.
- Old collections should be offered to other collectors or museums. These should not simply be thrown away – fossil collecting is not a sustainable activity.
- For those new to geology, it is advisable to join an amateur geological society. These societies provide regular field trips to places of geological interest and are conducted by experienced geologists.

Please also remember the Countryside Code. Further information at www.countrysideaccess.gov.uk/things_to_know/countryside_code

Finding fossils is not always simple. The easiest to spot are those free of rock or sitting exposed. Fossils can also be concealed in rocks and are only revealed by splitting the rocks. Only start extensive searching if you know the area contains fossiliferous rocks, otherwise you are causing a lot of needless damage. Look for clues in the area.

(a). A piece of limestone rock (with a mould of an ammonoid on its surface). The rock was found dislodged from an outcrop containing ammonoid fossils on its surface.

Most counties in Ireland have places in which fossils can be found. The localities named later are by no means exhaustive but they are among the commonest documented in the geological literature. This guide identifies the most common fossils found in Ireland. If, however, you want additional information on their identity you can access more detailed guides through a library or you could ask an expert in the geology department of a museum. Museums will often have national or local fossil collections, providing information

(b). When split open it revealed the cast and the mould (left) of an ammonoid.

on places to visit and the fossils you are likely to find.

Just a few words of encouragement: if your visits to the localities mentioned here prove unproductive, all is not lost. At least you will have seen the types of rock in which fossils can occur.

(c). Photo showing a plasticine cast (orange colour) made from the mould of the ammonoid. Remember not only casts, but also moulds, are fossils; splitting a suitable rock can be doubly productive.

The difficulty encountered in trying to locate fossils is compensated by a sense of achievement and satisfaction when fossils are found. Consider that it is possible that you might be the first person ever to see a particular specimen which lived millions of years ago.

FOSSILS FOUND
IN IRELAND

Example of a sponge fossil (weathered), whose scientific name is *Rhizopoterion cribrosum*, (carrot-shaped sponge), which was photographed in the Sponge Beds at Cloghfin Port, Islandmagee, Co. Antrim. The coin is 2.5 cm in diameter. [Photo: Mrs. R. Grainger, Belfast Geologists' Society.]

SPONGES
(Phylum: Porifera)

Time range: Early Cambrian to present-day.
Basic description:
These are the simplest of the multicelled animals. Their skeleton is internal and is composed of calcium carbonate ($CaCO_3$) or silica (SiO_2) spicules (spikes) or spongin (as in bath sponges). The spicules form the sponge's skeletal framework and can occur loose as fossils. They draw in water through pores on their surface, extract micro-organisms (for food) and oxygen (for breathing) from the water, and then expel it through an opening at their top. Sponges, today and in the past, are mainly marine, living in relatively clear water and inhabiting it at all depths. Most sponges that lived in the past do not differ greatly from present-day ones.

Localities where sponge fossils have been found:
- Cloghfin Port, Islandmagee, Co. Antrim.

Take the path from the end of Port Road down to the bay. Walk along the beach for about 100 m in a southerly direction. The outcrop containing sponge fossils ('Sponge Bed') forms a 'wall' about 2-3 m high and is situated, on the shore, between

Examples of sponge fossils

the greensand (dark green) and chalk. Abundant loose material containing sponges can be found along the shore. It is best accessed at low tide.
- Waterloo Bay, about 1 km north of Larne, Co. Antrim.

Again the Sponge Bed lies between the greensand and the chalk and lies about 50 m NE of the cottages. The bed is on the shore, dipping around 20°, is approximately 2-3 m thick and can be viewed at low tide. Note that a good portion of it can be covered by pebbles.

- Hillsport, Islandmagee, Co. Antrim, about 1km south of the entrance to the Gobbins path.
Present in slipped material on the beach.
- Portmuck (about 12 km from Whitehead), Co. Antrim.
Present in rocks at the base of the chalk – present in loose blocks on the beach.

In these localities the sponge fossils are hard to remove without damaging them – so best not even to try. Besides seeing them *in situ*, you could photograph them.

Coral fossils, the genus *Siphonodendron*, in the Carboniferous Limestone on the east side of Cuilcagh Mountain, Co. Fermanagh. (The head of the hammer is 20 cm long.) [Photo reproduced with the kind permission of the Director of the N.I. Geological Survey.]

CORALS
(Phylum: Coelenterata)

Time range: Ordovician to present-day.
Basic description:
In life corals consist of a soft part, called a polyp, and an external skeleton made of calcium carbonate, which is secreted by the polyp. Because polyps are composed of soft material they are, almost invariably, not preserved as fossils – just the hard skeletons occur as fossils. Polyps have tentacles, which are able to gather food and sting prey. Corals can be solitary (one polyp 'sitting' on a single skeleton) or colonial (a group of polyps, each one 'sitting' on a skeleton in contact with other skeletons). Two main groups of fossil coral can be found in Ireland – rugose corals (so called because of their wrinkled surfaces), and tabulate corals. The latter group became extinct at the end of the Permian Period and the former in the Early Triassic, to be replaced by a group called the scleractinians (pronounced "scleer-act-inians"), which are the main living group found today. All three groups were/are marine. Rugose corals were solitary or colonial, while tabulates were colonial.

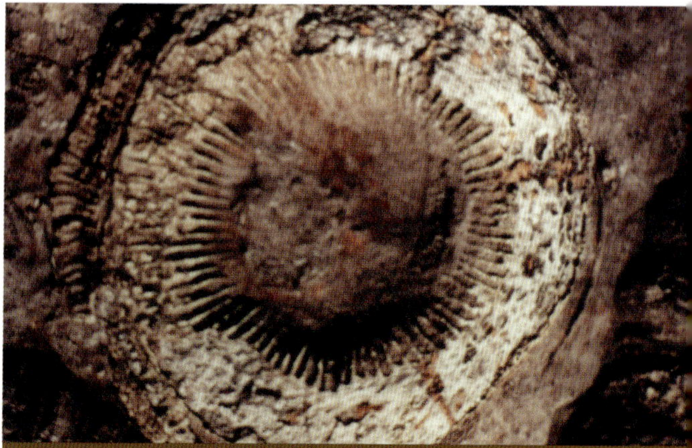

This example was seen in the Glencar Limestone exposure south of Streedagh Point, Co. Sligo.

Picture of a tabulate (colonial) coral fossil. This one is the genus *Michelinia*, which occurs in Carboniferous Limestone at Soldier's Point, near Cranfield, Co. Down.

Corals

Localities where coral fossils have been found:

- Quarry at Annacramph (on the road junction on the Loughgall Road, about 5 km NNE of Armagh city), Co. Armagh.

Fossils of many varieties of corals can be collected in the Carboniferous Limestone of this working quarry.

- Donaghadee harbour pier, Co. Down.

Coral fossils can be seen in the Carboniferous Limestone flagstones and are most obvious when the surface is wet. Note: *these are not to be tampered with*.

- At Portrane (about 20 km NNE of Dublin city), Co. Dublin.

Coral fossils occur in the Ordovician-age limestone found in the cliffs and on the rocky shore.

- Gortalughany (on the east side of Cuilcagh Mountain), Co. Fermanagh.

Branching rugose corals can be seen in the Carboniferous Limestone here.

- Streedagh Point to Rinnadoolish (4 km NW of Grange), Co. Sligo.

The beach exposure is littered with solitary horn–shaped coral fossils. This shore is normally safe but it can be dangerous in or after stormy weather if the Atlantic rollers are running, when

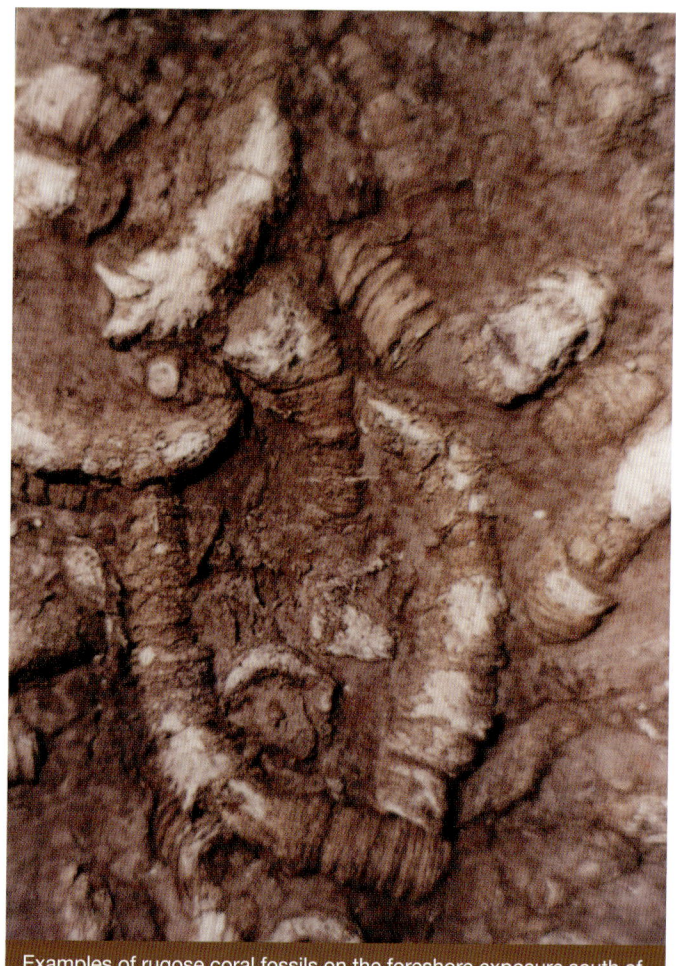
Examples of rugose coral fossils on the foreshore exposure south of Streedagh Point, Co. Sligo. [Photo: Robin Reid, England.]

Colonial coral in limestone, Donaghadee, Co. Down

the sea can rise suddenly right up to the low earth cliff behind the foreshore. So *take extreme care here.*
- Soldier's Point, Kilkeel, Co. Down.

The Cambrian trilobite, the genus *Elarthria*. Trilobites had walking legs but these are not usually fossilised. [Photo: Robin Reid, England.]

ARTHROPODS
(Phylum: Arthropoda)

Arthropods are the largest living animal phylum which today includes all insects, spiders and crustaceans, amongst others. The commonest arthropod fossils found in Ireland are the now extinct triolobites and the small crustaceans called ostracods which have been around from the Cambrian Period.

ARTHROPODS – Trilobites

Time range: Early Cambrian to Permian.
Basic description:
Tri-lob(e)-ites, which superficially resemble present-day wood-lice, are so called because their bodies are divided lengthwise into three parts – a central lobe and two side lobes. They had a hard external 'shell'. Trilobites shed this periodically during their lifetime, each shell being a potential fossil.

All of them possessed a respiratory, nervous, circulatory and reproductive system and they are amongst the oldest invertebrates. Most lived on the sea-floor, while some swam or floated; they were exclusively marine. They were at their most numerous during the

A selection of trilobite fossils. The fossils at the top and bottom of the image show the head section only.

ARTHROPODS – Trilobites

Ordovician Period, but what caused their extinction at the end of the Permian Period is unclear. Possible reasons include predation by the fishes, nautiloids and ammonoids or maybe a major environmental change.

Localities where trilobite fossils have been found:

- On the shore adjacent to the Castle Espie Quarries (about 3.5 km from Comber), Co. Down.

They have turned up in blocks of Carboniferous Limestone, but note that these are only accessible at low tide.

- At the Portrane shore (about 20 km NNE of Dublin city), Co. Dublin.

Fossils of trilobites occur along the cliffs and rocky shore in limestone of Ordovician age.

- Little River (about 210 m east of Slate Quarry Bridge), in the Pomeroy area, Co. Tyrone.

Here they have been found in silty mudstone in the banks of the river.

- Garrow Strand, Caher, Tramore, Co. Waterford.

Trilobites have been found in limestone of Ordovician age here.

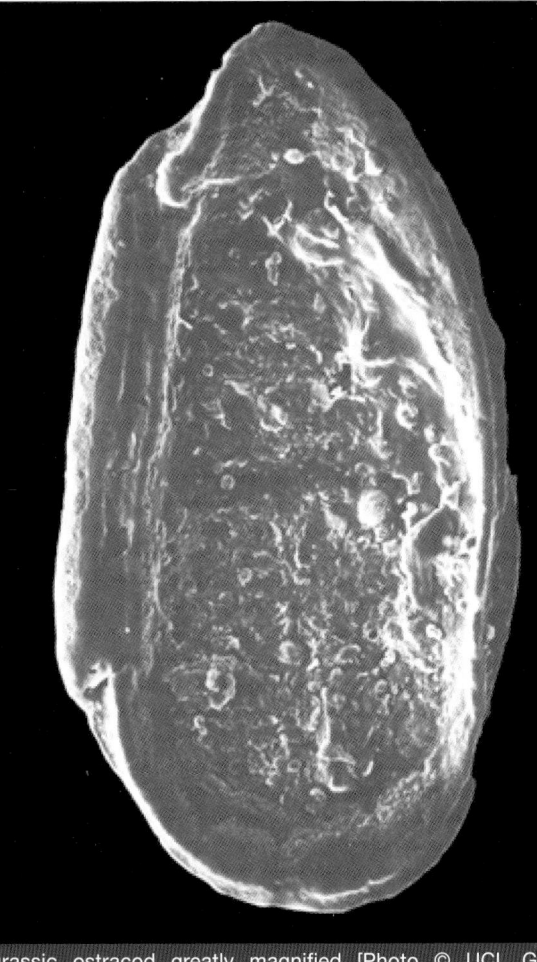

Jurassic ostracod greatly magnified [Photo © UCL Geology Collection.]

ARTHROPODS – Ostracods

Time range: Cambrian to present-day.
Basic description:
Ostracods are small soft-bodied animals enclosed by two shells (called valves). The shells are composed of chitinous material. They range in size from 0.5 mm to 1 cm in length and a microscope would be needed to study the minute types, which would be the majority. Many can be seen, however, unaided or using a hand-lens. Ostracods usually live in shallow seas, but some forms can inhabit fresh or brackish (partially salty) water.

Localities where ostracod fossils have been found:

- In the Lias Clay in Co. Antrim.

The Lias Clay is a dark-bluish, sticky, soft mixture of clay and shale, of Early Jurassic age. It is exposed at quite a few places in Co. Antrim and can contain bands of limestone. Where it is exposed, it lies below the greensand (if present) or, if not present, below the chalk. Some places to look are: the Waterloo shore, about 1 km from Larne, under the pebbles in the vicinity of the disused sewer

View of the clay landslip at the Minnis. The Lias Clay is the dark-bluish clay at approximately the centre of the landslip. It could be collected from the deposit on the shore. Warning: *do not attempt to climb this cliff, as the soft clay here is unstable.*

pipe (about 200 m south of cottages); on the beach opposite the Minnis landslip, which is about 15 km north of Larne, at the side of the Coast Road. Ostracod fossils are difficult to see *in situ*, but you could collect a small portion of the Lias Clay and bring it home for the experiment described on p. 94.

• In the Carboniferous dark grey mudstone, found at Portnaloub, about 5 km ENE of Ballycastle, Co. Antrim. Again you would need to

ARTHROPODS – Ostracods

collect a sample of this rock and bring it home to extract the ostracods.

- At Portrane (about 20 km NNE of Dublin city), Co. Dublin.

Ostracod fossils have been found in limestone of Ordovician age in the vicinity of the beach. Here they are silicified and they can be extracted from the limestone using undiluted vinegar which is available from most fish and chip shops. This experiment can take quite some time.

Examples of inarticulate ('hingeless' shelled) brachiopod fossils, the genus *Lingula*, which still live today. They were photographed *in situ* in Silurian red siltstone at Killary Bay, Co. Galway. [Photo published with the kind permission of the trustees of the Museums & Galleries of N. Ireland.]

BRACHIOPODS
(Phylum: Brachiopoda)

Time range: Cambrian to present-day.
Basic description:
Brachiopods have two shells, of unequal size, which contain the soft parts of the animal. In most species the shells are composed of calcium carbonate. In the more advanced forms (articulates) the shells are 'hinged', whereas in the less-developed types (the inarticulates) the shells are 'hingeless'. The valves (shells) open and shut by a system of muscles. When open they can absorb water and, using an internal structure, are able to extract food and oxygen from the water.

Today, and presumably in the past, brachiopods are almost exclusively marine – one exception being the genus *Lingula*, which can tolerate brackish water. Most have an aperture through which a fleshy stalk, called a pedicle, emerges to anchor the animal to the sea-bed. The small number without a pedicle were attached by cementing or embedded by spines, while some were not attached. Many groups of brachiopods became extinct at the end of the Permian Period and they have gradually declined in number since then. They are not as numerous today as in the geological past but, by studying living brachiopods, scientists can make deductions about fossilised ones.

The extinct brachiopod, genus *Spirifer*, which occurs in Northern Ireland Carboniferous Limestone.

Localities where brachiopod fossils have been found:

- Belshaw's Quarry National Nature Reserve, Bensons Road (about 5 km NW of Lisburn – can be accessed via the Lisburn Road, Belfast)
Brachiopods could be found in loose lumps of chalk here. But, because this is a disused quarry, do not remove any fossils seen *in situ*.
- Hillsport (about 4 km from Whitehead), Islandmagee, Co. Antrim.
In the greensand and chalk exposures, at this bay, brachiopod fossils have turned up.

Modern-day brachiopod found off Rathlin Island, Co. Antrim [Photo © Bernard Picton, Ulster Museum]

- Armagh city, Co. Armagh.

Fossils of brachiopods can be seen in the building stones of the museum and houses in Charlemont Place and in some of the paving stones in Charlemont Place. *These are not to be tampered with*.

- St John's Point (about 25 km WSW of Donegal town), Co. Donegal.

On the beaches here, brachiopod fossils can be found in the Carboniferous Limestone.

- Feltrim Hill Quarries (near Swords), Co. Dublin.

Brachiopod fossils (for example *Spirifer* and

Brachiopod fossils

Productus brachiopod, found in Ballyshannon Carboniferous Limestone at St John's Point, Co. Donegal. Coin is 2.5 cm in diameter. [Photo: Mrs R Grainger, Belfast Geologists' Society]

Productus) have been found in the Carboniferous Limestone here.
- Streedagh Point to Rinnadoolish (4 km NW of Grange), Co. Sligo.

See information under corals
- Killary Bay, Co. Galway.

Picture of (magnified) Carboniferous Limestone at Hook Head, Co. Wexford showing the net-like shape of a bryozoan (*Fenestella*) fossil. This genus became extinct at the end of the Permian Period. [Photo: Ulster Museum]

BRYOZOANS
(Phylum: Bryozoa)

Time range: Ordovician to present-day.
Basic description:
Bryozoans consist of minute animals called zooids which secrete their own protective individual external skeleton in which the animal lives. They live in colonies known as sea-mats, and their fossils, many of which have a net-like shape, represent their external skeletons or 'housing'. Zooids, because they are composed of soft tissue, are not fossilised – only the 'housing', which is made of hard material, is preserved.

The zooids have tentacles which enables them to collect food, in the form of micro-organisms, from the water. Although similar in some ways to polyps, zooids are more anatomically advanced than polyps. Bryozoans are all aquatic, living mostly in the sea. Living bryozoans cling to seaweeds, rocks or shells and this would have been the case in the past. Some of their fossils are found encrusting the shells of other fossils – for example sea-urchins.

The modern-day bryozoan *Electra pilosa* near the Maiden's, Larne, Co. Antrim [Photo © Bernard Picton, Ulster Museum]

Localities where bryozoan fossils have been found:

- Acheson Quarry (about 2 km SW of Killylea, situated on the Cavanapole Road, which is off the Kennedies Road), Co. Armagh.
Bryozoan fossils in the Carboniferous Limestone of this working quarry.
- Portrane (about 20 km NNE of Dublin city), Co. Dublin.
Fossils of bryozoans in the limestone of Ordovician age at the beach area.
- Ferriters Cove (just south of Sybil Point, western part of the Dingle Peninsula, about 6 km north of Dunquin), Co. Kerry.
Specimens of bryozoans have turned up in greenish/yellowish siltstone of Silurian age.
- Streedagh Point to Rinnadoolish (4 km NW of Grange), Co. Sligo.
See information under corals
- Hook Head, Co. Wexford.

A selection of gastropod fossils. Note that the ones at the top and bottom above do not have the familiar spiral shell – they could be mistaken for ammonoids – but gastropods do not have the suture lines seen in ammonoids. (Compare with photograph on p. 74)

MOLLUSCS
(Phylum: Mollusca)

Molluscs are a very large and diverse group of animals typically found in the sea and ranging from snails (e.g. periwinkles) and clams (e.g. mussels) to larger organisms such as squid and octopus. They are also a very ancient group, first appearing early in the Cambrian Period.

Members of the group include:
- Gastropods;
- Bivalves;
- Ammonoids (comprising Goniatites, Ceratites and Ammonites);
- Belemnites.

MOLLUSCS – Gastropods

Time range: Cambrian to present-day.
Basic description:
Known commonly as snails, gastropods are soft-bodied animals, which live inside a single shell composed of calcium carbonate. Shells can vary in size from 1 mm to 10cms, but some can be up to 50 cm in length. The majority crawl slowly on a 'foot' and inhabit the sea, fresh water and land. They feed on dead plants or animals while some are predators. Gastropods are at their

numerical peak at present times and were not widely distributed during the geological past. Their fossils are not abundant in Ireland.

Localities where gastropod fossils have been found:

- Belshaw's Quarry, Bensons Road (about 5 km NW of Lisburn – can be accessed from Belfast via the Lisburn Road), Co. Antrim.
Fossils of gastropods have been found in the Cretaceous Chalk of this quarry, but only collect from loose chalk samples.
- The facing stone of the Cecil Ward Building, 4-10 Linenhall Street, central Belfast.
The stone of this building, called Portland Roach, of Jurassic age, contains cavities that were once occupied by fossils – mostly gastropods. The fossils were composed of a form of calcium carbonate, called aragonite, which is relatively soluble. Obviously *there is to be no hammering here* but if you press a lump of plasticine into a cavity, and then carefully remove it, you could obtain the cast of the original (gastropod) fossil.
- Ferriters Cove (just south of Sybil Point, western part of the Dingle Peninsula, about 6 km north of Dunquin), Co. Kerry.
Gastropod fossils have turned up here in greenish/yellow siltstone of Silurian age.

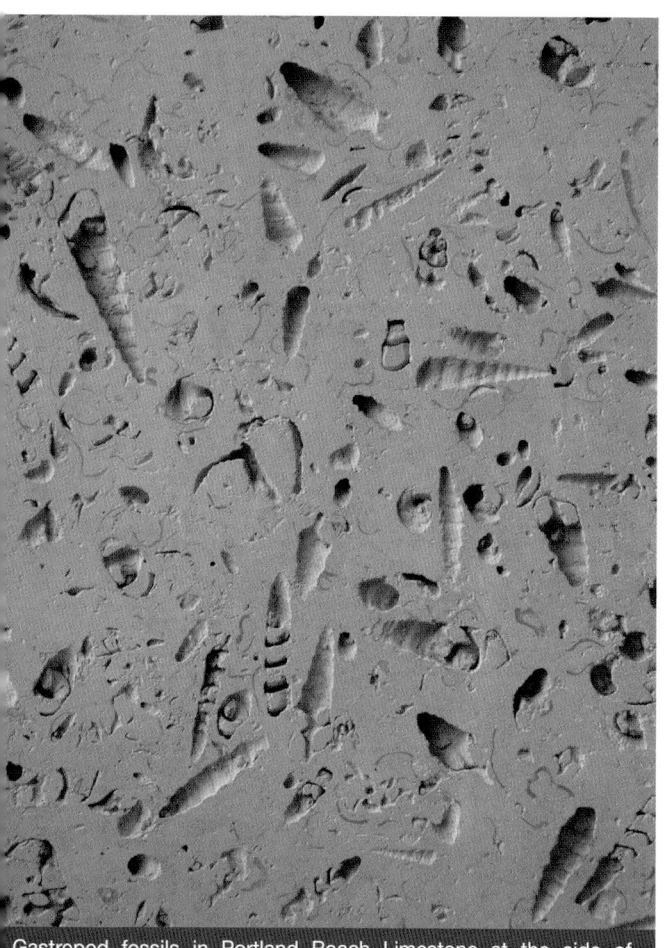

Gastropod fossils in Portland Roach Limestone at the side of the Cecil Ward Building, Linenhall Street, central Belfast. These gastropod fossils are known as Portland Screws.

A collection of bivalve fossils. [Photo © Ulster Museum]

MOLLUSCS – Bivalves

Time range: Middle Cambrian to present day.
Basic description:
Also called lamellibranchs (pronounced "lamelly-branks"), bivalves have their soft parts residing between two shells (valves) composed of calcium carbonate and which, in most cases, are almost identical (but mirror images of each other). The shells are 'hinged' and can open and close. Shells can vary in size from 0.5-10 cm but some can be as long as 50 cm.

All bivalves are aquatic, living mostly in the sea, and they absorb water, from which they extract food and oxygen. They live on the bottom (e.g. oysters) or buried in sediments (e.g. cockles) while some can swim short distances across the sea-floor by snapping their shells (e.g. scallops). Most of the shells on our beaches today are from bivalves but these are too recent to be fossils. Bivalves are more numerous today than in the geological past and by studying modern forms scientists can come to a better understanding of fossil forms.

Gryphaea bivalve fossils

Localities where bivalve fossils have been found:

- Portmuck (about 12 km from Whitehead), Co. Antrim.

In loose rocks along shore, north of the car park. Fragments of *Inoceramus* (a dinner plate-sized bivalve) are common in the greensand. The green colour of this rock is often obscured by weathering. If, however, you scratch the surface (say with a pebble), the green colour is revealed.

- Waterloo shore (about 1 km north of Larne), Co. Antrim.

Bivalves (e.g. *Gryphaea*) in the Lias Clay. Best to search among the pebbles just south of the cottages – particularly the area around the disused pipe.

- Malahide beach (about 14 km NNE of Dublin city), Co. Dublin.

Fossils of bivalves have been found in Carboniferous Limestone in the vicinity of the beach.

- Coolcullen (about 5 km SW of Bilboa), Co. Laois.

In the tip above Millford House, bivalve fossils have been found in the Carboniferous Limestone.

A selection of ammonoid fossils

MOLLUSCS – Ammonoids

Goniatites
Time range: Early Devonian to Late Permian.
Ammonites
Time range: Early Jurassic to Late Cretaceous.

Basic description:
Collectively goniatites, ceratites and ammonites are called ammonoids. Ceratites, which lived in the Triassic Period, do not occur in Ireland and are not covered here. Both goniatites and ammonites had external shells, composed of calcium carbonate, with the main soft parts protruding from the last open chamber of the shell. The separate turns of the shell are called 'whorls', which become bigger from the centre outward. They had a distinct head, unlike say the bivalves, and tentacles surrounded the mouth region. Both resemble the present-day *Nautilus* and they would have evolved from nautiloids. By studying the present-day *Nautilus* we can speculate on the now-extinct goniatites and ammonites. Ammonoids were strictly marine and swam with their shell in the vertical plane, moving by using their tentacles or by shooting out a jet of water. They could also control their buoyancy by varying the amount of gas (which

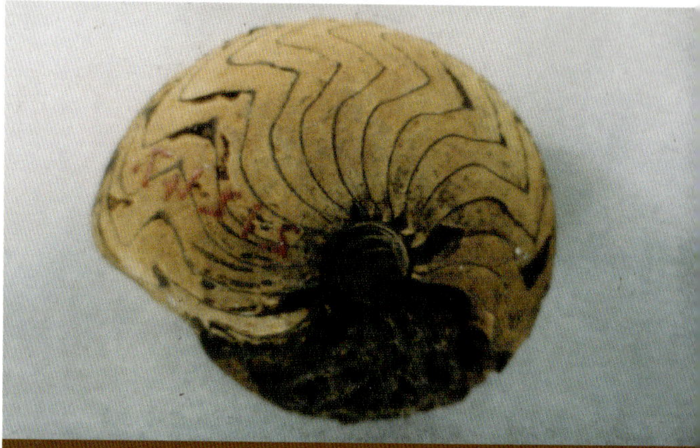

A goniatite fossil showing angular suture lines [Photo: Robin Reid, England.]

An ammonite fossil showing more complex suture lines. [Photo: Robin Reid, England.]

they extracted from the sea water) in their shell. We can distinguish goniatites from ammonites by their suture lines, which are seen in fossils where the thin outer shell has been worn away or by carefully removing part of it. Goniatites have angular or curved suture lines while ammonites have more complex ones. But, there are some exceptions to this.

Localities where goniatite and ammonite fossils have been found:

- The Minnis north foreshore (on Coast Road, about 15 km north of Larne, just north of Drumnagreagh), Co. Antrim.

Fossils of ammonites, some of which could be pyritised, could be collected from the clay deposit on the shore, in the vicinity of the drain-pipe. *Do not attempt to climb the landslip on the opposite side of the road.*

- Cliffs of Moher (about 5 km NNW of Liscannor), Co. Clare.

Goniatites of Carboniferous age can be seen in the exposed rocks at the side of the public path leading from the village of Doolin to the top of the cliffs. *Do not attempt to climb these cliffs.*

- Carmean Limestone Quarry (near Moneymore), Co. Londonderry.

From the base of the Cretaceous rocks in this quarry, ammonite fossils have been found.
- Waterloo
- Portrush (*see p. 12*)

MOLLUSCS – Belemnites

Time range: Late Carboniferous to Early Palaeogene.

Basic description:
Belemnites had a bullet-shaped calcareous internal shell, called a 'guard', enclosed by a soft body. The guard is often the only part fossilised and, when it is broken, it usually shows a radial structure in cross-section. Present-day squids closely resemble belemnites. They moved/swam by either using their fins or by shooting out water. Belemnites were most numerous during the Jurassic and Cretaceous Periods.

Localities where belemnite fossils have been found:

Belemnites are widespread in the Cretaceous Chalk – some specific localties are:
- Waterloo shore (about 1 km north of Larne), Co. Antrim.

If you look among the pebbles overlying the

A collection of belemnite fossils

Belemnite with the rock it was preserved in.

The belemnite, genus *Belemnitella*, which is common in the Northern Ireland Chalk.

MOLLUSCS – Belemnites

Lias Clay on the shore, you could find belemnite fossils. Look particularly at the area, just south of the cottages, around the disused pipe.
- Minnis north foreshore (about 15 km north of Larne, on the Coast Road), Co. Antrim.

Examine the clay deposit on the shore, just opposite the landslip. If you found any belemnite fossils here, you could retain them.
- Carmean Limestone Quarry (near Moneymore), Co. Londonderry.

Belemnites have been found in the Cretaceous Chalk of this working quarry.

A selection of sea-urchin fossils

ECHINODERMS
(Phylum: Echinodermata)

The term echinoderm refers to spiny skin, typical of these animals. They include sea-urchins, crinoids (sea lilies), starfish and brittle stars. The first two are covered in this section.

ECHINODERMS – Sea-urchins

Time range: Ordovician to present-day.
Basic description:
Often called echinoids, sea-urchins are free-moving marine animals with a calcareous shell, which bears spines, and is covered by a skin. The movable spines are for protection and can be employed for walking or burrowing. Usually the spines are not preserved on fossils, while the main shell can be globe-like, heart-shaped or disc-like in shape. They have a typical radiating pattern of five 'bands', called ambulacra, containing tiny pores from which 'tube-feet' protrude to enable them to cling to firm surfaces and, in some, can assist with feeding, breathing or burrowing.

Sea-urchins, like crinoids, have a 'water vascular system', which is unique in the animal kingdom. Water, instead of blood, circulates around their bodies carrying food and oxygen. It is

Fossil of the sea-urchin, genus *Palaechinus*, from the Carboniferous Ben Bulben Shale, Co. Sligo. It did not survive the Permian extinctions. [Photo: Robin Reid, England.]

roughly equivalent to the cardio-vascular system in higher animals. The sea-urchins suffered badly in the Permian extinctions but survivors went on to flourish, reaching a numerical peak towards the end of the Cretaceous, after which numbers were again reduced. Today, the edible sea-urchin, *Echinus*, lives along rocky Irish coasts.

A fossil specimen, the genus *Micraster*, which can be found at White Park Bay, Co. Antrim. Each one of the five radiating 'sunken' areas is an ambulacrum. It was a burrowing sea-urchin which lived during the Late Cretaceous.

Localities where sea-urchin fossils have been found:

- Cloghfin Port (about 2 km from Whitehead), Islandmagee, Co. Antrim.

Here fossils of sea-urchins have turned up in the chalk (vertical exposure).

- White Park Bay (about 81 km from Larne), Co. Antrim.

In the chalk, past the basalt sea stacks, sea-urchin fossils have been found.

- Limestone Quarry at 1079 Upper Crumlin Road (about 6 km from Carlisle Circus, on R.H.S.), north Belfast.

The Cretaceous Chalk in this working quarry has yielded sea-urchin fossils. Examine especially loose chalk rocks.

- Carmean Limestone Quarry (near Moneymore), Co. Londonderry.

Look at the chalk exposures in this working quarry for specimens of sea-urchin fossils.

- Hillsport, Islandmagee, Co. Antrim.

Present in the slipped material on the beach about 1 km south of the entrance to the Gobbins path.

ECHINODERMS – Crinoids

Time range: Ordovician to present-day.
Basic description:
There are two types of crinoid animals, both of which are marine – a stemmed variety that is attached to the sea-floor and a swimming variety. In very simple terms, the swimming ones are similar to the stemmed types except they have no stems. Most fossil crinoids are from the stemmed types and usually consist of small 'bones', called ossicles, from their flexible

Examples of fossilised crinoid ossicles found in shaly limestone at the Acheson Quarry. Co. Armagh. [Photo: Dr. J. Preston, Belfast]

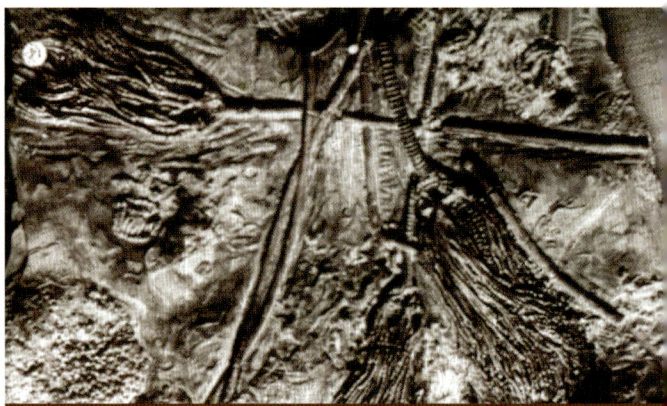

A limestone of Carboniferous age composed mostly of crinoid fossils. Such limestones are called crinoidal limestones.

Crinoid stems and 'arms'. [Photo © Ulster Museum]

ECHINODERMS – Crinoids

stems and arms. These are composed of calcium carbonate. Because they look like plants, the stemmed crinoids are sometimes called 'sea lilies'. The main soft parts of the animal reside in a cup, also called a calyx, and have five, or multiples of five, branching arms which sweep microscopic food particles from the sea water into the mouth which sits at the top of the cup. Crinoids were most numerous in the Devonian but whole groups became extinct at the end of the Permian. In the Triassic numbers increased to some degree. Between the Ordovician and Permian only the stemmed types were around, with the swimming ones evolving later. Although crinoids exist today, they are not very numerous with the swimming ones more common than the stemmed types.

Localities where crinoid fossils have been found:

- Acheson Quarry (about 2 km SW of Killylea, on the Cavanapole Road, which is off the Kennedies Road), Co. Armagh.

Crinoid ossicle fossils occur in the Carboniferous Limestone of this working quarry.

- Gortalughany (on the east side of Cuilcagh Mountain), Co. Fermanagh.

Crinoid fossils

Crinoids are common in the Carboniferous Limestone here.

- St John's Point (25 km WSW of Donegal town), Co. Donegal.

On the beach areas, the Carboniferous Limestone has yielded fossils of crinoid ossicles.

- Loughshinny (about 4 km north of Rush), Co. Dublin.

Fossils of crinoids can occur in the Carboniferous Limestone (north of pier).

- Newton Head, Raheen, Passage East, Co. Waterford.

Crinoids of Ordovician age have been found here.

- Streedagh Point to Rinnadoolish (4 km NW of Grange), Co. Sligo.

See information under corals

GRAPTOLITES
(Phylum: Hemichordata)

Time range: Early Ordovician to Early Devonian.
Basic description:
Graptolites are in the phylum (major group) Hemichordata (also called hemichordates) because they are very slightly similar to vertebrates, which are also called chordates. Each fossil is an outer skeleton of a colony of minute animals called zooids, each one residing in a cup. Zooids, because they only have soft parts,

Graptolites fossils. The serrations on the 'branches' represent the cups, where the zooids lived.

are not fossilised. The tiny cups were situated in rows along one or more 'branches' called stipes. Graptolite skeletons were made of an insoluble protein and are preserved as dark carbonised impressions or, sometimes, as whitish films. The dark impressions show a different reflectivity to light than the dark rock surfaces they are found on and so can be quite easily seen. Their fossils often resemble pencil scribbles and indeed their name comes from the Greek *graptos*, meaning 'written', and *lithos*, meaning 'rock', refering to their appearance. They are thought to have

Graptolite fossils (like pencil scribbles) in black shale

floated in seas, attached by a thread probably to seaweeds. Because they are now long extinct, scientists can only conjecture about their mode of life. In the Ordovician, graptolites were at their numerical peak and their complete extinction in the Devonian might have been due to predation by fishes, which proliferated in the seas at that time.

Locality where graptolite fossils have been found:

- Coalpit Bay, known locally as Recreation Bay (about 1 km from Donaghadee), Co. Down.

This is one of the best places in Ireland for graptolite fossils. There are two main places here: (1) in black shale, of Ordovician age, on the most southerly of the two rocky peninsulas in the centre of the bay and (2) in black shales, of Silurian age, at the 'old pit' under a small cliff at the southern (Millisle) side of the bay. The Silurian rocks here yield more graptolite fossils than the Ordovician ones.

EXPERIMENTS TO TRY AT HOME

Experiment to obtain ostracod fossils.

One way to extract ostracod fossils is to take a handful of the soft Lias Clay in Co. Antrim, deposit it in a plastic bag and bring it home. Add water and then boil the sample in a suitable container. A quarter teaspoonful of washing soda could be added. The clay particles will go into suspension while the heavier ostracod fossils, if present, will fall to the bottom. Carefully decant off the liquid containing the clay. Repeat this procedure as many times as necessary to remove the clay. Allow the residue to dry then, using a fine paint brush with a damp tip, remove the individual ostracod or other fossils. A strong hand-lens will help distinguish these microfossils.

Experiment to obtain fossils of small fish bones/teeth from greensand.

Remove a small sample of greensand from the loose material on the shore at: Portmuck, Islandmagee, about 150 m north of the car park and the Waterloo shore, NE of the cottages. Break into 2cm cubes and place into a glass container. Cover with household vinegar or stronger 'Chip Shop' vinegar. Leave for 2-3 days and then pour off liquid. Top-up with fresh vinegar and repeat process until all the greensand disintegrates (around 2-3 weeks). Gently wash the residue a couple of times with water to remove any (white) organic salts. When residue settles, pour off the liquid and leave the green residue to (air) dry for a few days. Pour the dry residue onto white paper and carefully sift through it, looking out for fossils such as small fish bones and fish teeth. These fossils can vary in size from 0.5-10 mm so a hand-lens will be helpful. The small fish bones and teeth are usually shiny in appearance. If you are very lucky you may find fossils of sharks' teeth.

Fossils of sharks' teeth

ACKNOWLEDGEMENTS

I am greatly indebted to Robin Reid and Dr. J. Preston for enlightening me about palaeontology, and other branches of geology, over the years. Others to whom I owe thanks for educating me in the subject of geology are: Professor Tony Bazley, Phil Doughty, Rosalie Grainger, Dr. A. Jeram, Pat McBride, Peter Millar, Dr. W. I. Mitchell, Dr. N. Moles, Professor J. Parnell, Dr. A. Ruffell, Ralph Semple and Dr. M. J. Simms. As the study of fossils and the subject of biology are inextricably linked, it would be relevant here to express thanks to my first, and best, biology teacher at the C.B.S. in Belfast: Davy Rice. Lastly, I am exceedingly grateful to the Environment and Heritage Service, Department of the Environment, courtesy of Mr Ian Enlander, for their significant grant towards publication costs and editorial input.

FURTHER READING

Allaby, A. and M. (1999). *Dictionary of Earth Sciences*. Oxford University Press, Oxford.

Kennan, P.S. (1995). *Written in Stone*. Geological Survey of Ireland.

Lyle, P. (2003). *The North of Ireland*. Terra Publishing, Harpenden, England.

McKeever, P.J. (1999). *A Story Through Time. The Formation of the Scenic Landscapes of Ireland [North]*. Geological Survey of Ireland and N. Ireland Geological Survey.

Mitchell, W.I. (2004). *The Geology of Northern Ireland. Our Natural Foundation*. The N. Ireland Geological Survey.

Parkes, M.A. and Sleeman, A.G. (1997). *Catalogue of the Type, Figured and Cited Fossils in the Geological Survey of Ireland*. Geological Survey of Ireland.

Rhodes, F.H.T.; Zim, H.S. and Shaffer, P.R. (1990). *Fossils – A Guide To Prehistoric Life*. Golden Books, New York.

Semple, T.R. (1996). *The Geology of the Borough of Larne*. Larne Borough Council, Co. Antrim.